# TERRORS OF THE TRIASSIC

by Louise Nelson

Minneapolis, Minnesota

**Credits**: All images are courtesy of Shutterstock.com, unless otherwise specified. With thanks to Getty Images, Thinkstock Photo, and iStockphoto. Cover – Warpaint, Julia-art, Michael Rosskothen, Wetzkaz Graphics, Nikulina Tatiana. Images used on every page – Julia-art, Wetzkaz Graphics, Nikulina Tatiana. 2 – Dotted Yeti. 4–5 – Catmando, Dotted Yeti, Orla. 6–7 – Dotted Yeti. 8–9 – Elenarts, Kostiantyn Ivanyshen, YuRi Photolife. 10–11 – Andreas Meyer, Kostiantyn Ivanyshen, Sk_Advance studio. 12–13 – Dotted Yeti, Sk_Advance studio. 14–15 – Adriana Sulugiuc, Catmando, Elenarts, Sk_Advance studio. 16–17 – Sk_Advance studio, Catmando. 18–19 – Agus_Gatam, Danny Ye, Pao W. 20–21 – Gorodenkoff, Rafael Trafaniuc. 22–23 – DanielFreyr, Orla.

Library of Congress Cataloging-in-Publication Data is available at www.loc.gov or upon request from the publisher.

ISBN: 979-8-88509-366-8 (hardcover)
ISBN: 979-8-88509-488-7 (paperback)
ISBN: 979-8-88509-603-4 (ebook)

© 2023 Booklife Publishing
This edition is published by arrangement with Booklife Publishing.

North American adaptations © 2023 Bearport Publishing Company. All rights reserved. No part of this publication may be reproduced in whole or in part, stored in any retrieval system, or transmitted in any form or by any means, electronic, mechanical, photocopying, recording, or otherwise, without written permission from the publisher.

For more information, write to Bearport Publishing, 5357 Penn Avenue South, Minneapolis, MN 55419.

# CONTENTS

The Time of Dinosaurs . . . . . . . . . . . . 4
The Triassic Period . . . . . . . . . . . . . . . . 6
Dinosaurs of the Triassic . . . . . . . . . . . 8
Not a Dino . . . . . . . . . . . . . . . . . . . . . . 10
How Do We Know? . . . . . . . . . . . . . . . 12
*Lystrosaurus* . . . . . . . . . . . . . . . . . . . 14
*Tanystropheus* . . . . . . . . . . . . . . . . . 16
*Desmatosuchus* . . . . . . . . . . . . . . . . 18
*Nothosaurus* . . . . . . . . . . . . . . . . . . 20
End of the Triassic . . . . . . . . . . . . . . . 22
Glossary . . . . . . . . . . . . . . . . . . . . . . . 24
Index . . . . . . . . . . . . . . . . . . . . . . . . . .24

# THE TIME OF DINOSAURS

Triassic

Long, long ago, very different creatures wandered Earth. Some had big bodies, terrifying teeth, or terrific tails. They were dinosaurs!

Dinosaurs lived on our planet for about 165 million years. This part of the past is known as the Mesozoic Era. It includes the Triassic, Jurassic, and Cretaceous periods.

Jurassic

Cretaceous

There were different dinos during different periods.

# THE TRIASSIC PERIOD

*This map shows Earth during the Triassic.*

During the Triassic period, Earth did not have separate **continents**. Instead, it was one big area of land called Pangea.

The Triassic period began after something caused the **extinction** of most plants and animals. Some of the animals that survived changed to become dinosaurs.

The Triassic lasted from 252 to 201 million years ago.

# DINOSAURS OF THE TRIASSIC

Coelophysis

The oldest dinosaur **fossils** come from the Triassic period. Most of these dinosaurs were small and walked on two legs. They are known as theropods.

*Coelophysis* is one kind of theropod.

# NOT A DINO

Many dinosaurs lived during the Triassic period. But other creatures did, too.

Dinosaurs are a specific group of animals. All dinosaurs are **reptiles**. But dinos have some differences from other reptiles.

Herrerasaurus

Non-dino reptiles have legs that come out from the sides of their bodies. Dino legs were directly under their bodies.

A gecko lizard

There are still many reptiles on Earth today, including lizards and crocodiles.

11

# HOW DO WE KNOW?

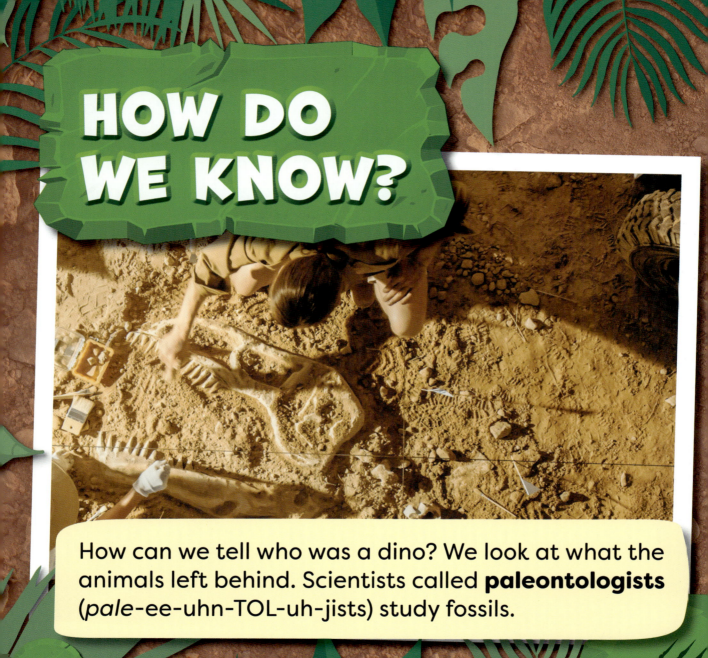

How can we tell who was a dino? We look at what the animals left behind. Scientists called **paleontologists** (*pale*-ee-uhn-TOL-uh-jists) study fossils.

# LYSTROSAURUS
(liss-tro-SOR-us)

Is that a dinosaur?

*Lystrosaurus* lived in the early Triassic. Scientists have found many of its fossils.

## A Quick Look

**Wet and Dry**
Some scientists think *Lystrosaurus* could have lived both on land and in water.

**Plant Eater**
You don't have to worry about being eaten by this plant-loving animal!

**Prehistoric Pig**
*Lystrosaurus* is sometimes called lizard-pig.

This animal was NOT a dinosaur.

15

# TANYSTROPHEUS
(tan-ee-STRO-fee-us)

What about that? Is it a dino?

*Tanystropheus* had a neck that was longer than its body and tail together!

16

## A Quick Look

### Water Walker
Tanystropheus lived mostly in or near water. It probably walked in water.

### Meat Eater
This big creature ate fish and other small animals.

### Neck or Wings?
Tanystropheus' neck has so many bones that scientists first thought they were wings.

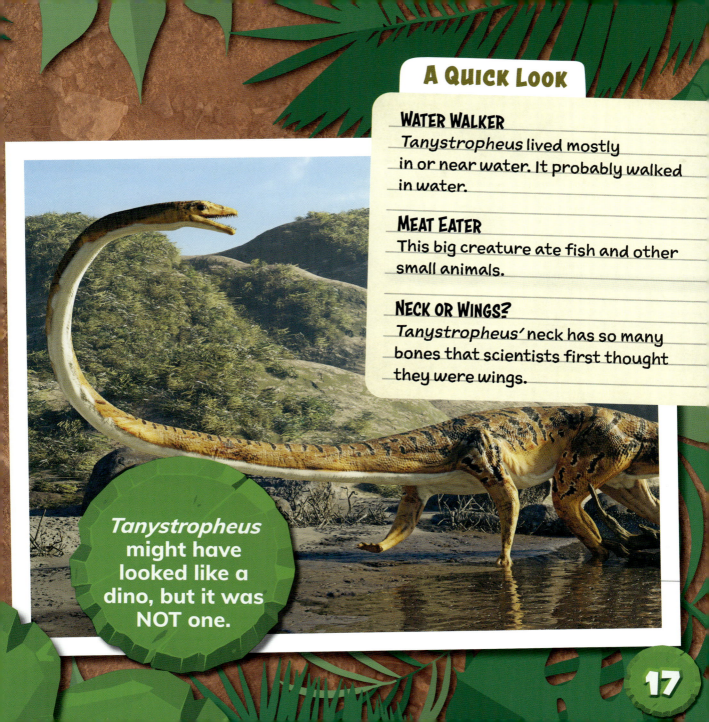

*Tanystropheus* might have looked like a dino, but it was NOT one.

## A Quick Look

**Tough Skin**
*Desmatosuchus'* hard skin was similar to some dino skin.

**Plant Eater**
This creature did not eat meat.

**As Long as a Car**
*Desmatosuchus* grew as long as a small car.

This animal was NOT a dino. It was related to today's crocodiles.

This animal was related to lizards and snakes. It was NOT a dinosaur.

## A Quick Look

### From Land to Water
*Nothosaurus* lived on land at first. Over many years, it **adapted** to live in oceans, too.

### Meat Eater
This creature ate fish and other animals.

### Teeth Trap
*Nothosaurus'* teeth acted like a trap for slippery **prey**!

# END OF THE TRIASSIC

The Triassic period ended almost as it started. Scientists think a lot of huge **volcanoes** exploded, causing many plants and animals to die.

Not everything was destroyed at the end of the Triassic. Many creatures, both dinosaurs and non-dinos, survived. They continued to live into the Jurassic period.

# GLOSSARY

**adapted** changed over time to fit its surroundings better

**continents** the world's seven large land masses

**extinction** death of a whole group of plants or animals

**fossils** bones, teeth, or other things left behind from life long ago

**paleontologists** scientists who study fossils to find out about life in the past

**prey** an animal that is hunted for food

**reptiles** cold-blooded animals that breathe air and have scaly skin

**volcanoes** mountains that can send out rocks, ash, and lava in sudden explosions

# INDEX

**continents** 6
**Cretaceous period** 5
**extinction** 7
**fish** 17, 21
**fossils** 8, 12–14
**Jurassic period** 5, 23
**lizards** 11, 15, 21
**paleontologists** 12–13
**reptiles** 10–11
**volcanoes** 22